Why was He Chosen?

(A Life of Prophet Muhammad)

Sadhu Prasad

Table of Contents

.... 1

Chapter 1 : Birth of Muhammad 7

Chapter 2 : Marriages of Muhammad.....13 13

2.1. Pre-Revelation Marriage.. 14

2.2. Post-Revelation Marriages 18

Chapter 3 : The Calling... 22

Chapter 4 : The Revelation..27

Chapter 5: Sharing his Revelation 30

Chapter 6: Trials and Tribulations....................................34

Chapter 7: The Hijrah 38

Chapter 8 : The Battles 41

8.1 Bàttle of Badr 44

8.2 Battle of Uhud...47

8.3 Battle of Khandaq..50

8.4 Conquest of Mecca...52

8.5 Battle of Hunayn..55

Chapter 9: The Legacy...58

Chapter 10 : Why Muhammad was Chosen?.....................61

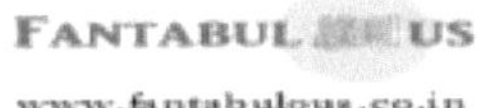

Publisher
Fantabulous Publishers India
www.fantabulous.co.in[1]

Edition: 2024

---

1. http://www.fantabulous.co.in

Why was He Chosen?
Penned by Sadhu Prasad
Published by Fantabulous Publishers India

Preface

In the vast expanse of human history, certain figures emerge whose lives transcend the boundaries of time and space, leaving an indelible mark on the tapestry of civilization. Among these luminaries stands Prophet Muhammad, a man whose legacy continues to resonate with millions around the world centuries after his earthly journey came to an end.

In this book, we embark on a journey through the life, teachings, and legacy of Prophet Muhammad, exploring the myriad facets of his character, the depth of his wisdom, and the profound impact of his message on the course of history. From his humble beginnings in the Arabian Peninsula to his role as the final messenger of God, we delve into the life of a man who embodies the highest ideals of compassion, justice, and spiritual enlightenment.

Through a rich tapestry of stories, anecdotes, and historical accounts, we uncover the remarkable journey of a man who transformed the world with his teachings of monotheism, social justice, and moral integrity. From his encounters with adversity and persecution to his triumphs on the battlefield and in the hearts of his followers, we witness the unfolding drama of a life guided by divine revelation and unwavering faith.

But this book is more than just a recounting of historical events; it is a testament to the enduring legacy of Prophet Muhammad and the timeless wisdom of his teachings. As we journey through the pages of this book, we are invited to reflect on the profound lessons and insights that Muhammad's life offers us, and to contemplate the relevance of his message in our own lives and times.

In an age marked by uncertainty, division, and strife, the life of Prophet Muhammad serves as a beacon of hope and guidance, illuminating the path towards a world characterized by compassion, justice, and peace. As we immerse ourselves in his story, we are reminded of the transformative power of faith, forgiveness, and love—the same qualities that defined Muhammad's life and continue to inspire countless millions around the world today.

So join me on this journey through the life and legacy of Prophet Muhammad—a journey that promises to enlighten, inspire, and uplift us as we discover the timeless wisdom of a man whose message continues to resonate with the hearts of humanity across the ages.

Warm Regards

Sadhu Prasad

Chapter 1 : Birth of Muhammad

In the heart of the Arabian Peninsula, amidst the shifting sands and ancient trade routes, there existed a city that would become the cradle of a new era—the city of Mecca. It was here, in the year 570 CE, that a child was born who would one day shape the course of human history. His name was Muhammad.

Muhammad's early years were not easy, a small boy had to face tremendous tragedy of his life. Before he even took his first breath, fate had already dealt him a heavy blow. His father, Abdullah, passed away before his birth, leaving him fatherless before he even entered the world. And when Muhammad was just six years old, he suffered another devastating loss—his mother, Amina, passed away, leaving him orphaned at a tender age.

The loss of Muhammad's father and mother at a young age can indeed be seen as a test of his resilience, faith, and character. In Islamic belief, trials and tribulations are often viewed as opportunities for personal growth and spiritual development. While the loss of his parents undoubtedly brought Muhammad profound grief and hardship, it also served to shape him into the compassionate and empathetic leader he would become.

For Muhammad, the early loss of his parents fostered a sense of humility and empathy for others who faced similar struggles. It allowed him to connect with the marginalized and downtrodden, as he knew firsthand what it was like to experience loss and adversity. This empathy would later inform his teachings on social justice and compassion, as he emphasized the importance of caring for the vulnerable members of society.

Additionally, the trials Muhammad faced early in life prepared him for the challenges he would encounter later as the messenger of God. His experiences of hardship and loss strengthened his resolve and deepened his faith, enabling him to withstand persecution and adversity with unwavering determination.

Again, In Islamic theology, believers are taught to view trials and tribulations as tests from God, opportunities to demonstrate patience, perseverance, and trust in His divine plan. For Muhammad, the loss of his parents was undoubtedly a test of his faith and resilience, but it also served to strengthen his connection to God and prepare him for the monumental task that lay ahead. Through his unwavering faith and steadfast determination, Muhammad emerged from these trials as a beacon of hope and guidance for believers around the world.

Talking more about his early days, amidst the darkness of loss of his parents, there was a glimmer of light. Muhammad was taken in by his grandfather, Abdul-Muttalib, a respected elder in the community who showered him with love and care. Under his grandfather's watchful eye, Muhammad grew strong and resilient, his spirit undimmed by the hardships he had endured.

Yet, fate was not finished with him yet. When Muhammad was still a young boy, his grandfather too passed away, leaving him once again adrift in a world filled with uncertainty. Death of his grandparent Abdul-Muttalib, undoubtedly created a significant emotional burden for him. Losing loved ones at such a young age can be incredibly challenging, leaving individuals feeling alone, vulnerable, and questioning why such hardships occur.

But as one door closed, another opened, and Muhammad found solace in the loving embrace of his uncle, Abu Talib-brother of Muhammad's father.

Abu Talib, played a significant role in raising and supporting Muhammad after the death of Muhammad's grandfather, Abdul-Muttalib. Abu Talib was not only Muhammad's guardian but also his protector and mentor, providing him with guidance, love, and stability during his formative years.

He welcomed Muhammad into his home and provided him with a nurturing environment in which to grow and thrive. Abu Talib's protection shielded Muhammad from the hardships of life as an orphan and ensured that he received the care and support he needed during his youth.

He instilled in Muhammad the principles of honesty, integrity, and compassion, which would later become hallmarks of Muhammad's character. Abu Talib's wisdom and guidance helped shape Muhammad into the man he would become, laying the foundation for his future role as the messenger of God.

As Muhammad grew older, Abu Talib provided him with opportunities to develop skills and gain experience. He involved Muhammad in the family trade caravan business, exposing him to the world of commerce and providing him with valuable lessons in entrepreneurship and diplomacy. Through these experiences, Muhammad honed his abilities as a trader and negotiator, preparing him for the challenges he would face later in life.

Also, Abu Talib stood by Muhammad through thick and thin, offering unwavering support and encouragement, particularly during times of adversity. One instance for the support in adversity is, when Muhammad faced opposition and persecution from the Quraysh tribe of Mecca due to his message of monotheism, Abu Talib remained a steadfast ally, providing protection and refuge for his nephew (More will be discussed in coming chapters). Despite the pressures and threats he faced from his own tribe, Abu Talib refused to abandon Muhammad, demonstrating his deep love and loyalty towards him.

In summary, Abu Talib played a crucial role in Muhammad's upbringing, providing him with love, guidance, and support throughout his formative years. His role as Muhammad's guardian, mentor, and protector helped shape Muhammad's character and prepared him for the momentous task that lay ahead as the messenger of God.

Under his uncle's guardianship, Muhammad flourished, his curious mind eager to explore the world around him. He spent his days wandering the bustling streets of Mecca, marveling at the sights and sounds of the vibrant city. And as he grew older, he began to take on responsibilities befitting his age, helping his uncle with the family's trade caravan and learning the ways of the merchant.

Therefore, Muhammad's early life was marked by hardship, resilience, and a deep sense of introspection. Raised as an orphan in the bustling city of Mecca, he experienced loss and adversity from a young age. Despite these challenges, Muhammad exhibited remarkable strength of character and a keen sense of empathy for those around him.

While, growing up in Mecca, Muhammad witnessed the stark inequalities that existed within society. The city was a hub of trade and commerce, but it was also plagued by social injustices and tribal rivalries. Muhammad keenly felt the plight of the marginalized and disenfranchised, and he harbored a deep-seated desire to alleviate their suffering.

As he matured, Muhammad began to take on responsibilities within his community, working as a shepherd and later as a merchant. These experiences exposed him to the harsh realities of life in 7th-century Arabia, but they also instilled in him a sense of resilience and resourcefulness.

Despite his outward success as a merchant, Muhammad's heart remained restless. He often sought solace in the quiet solitude of the desert, retreating to the Cave of Hira to meditate and reflect on the mysteries of existence. It was during one of these solitary retreats that Muhammad received his first revelation—an experience that would forever alter the course of his life.

But amidst the hustle and bustle of everyday life, there was always a sense of something greater stirring within Muhammad—a sense of purpose that seemed to beckon him towards a destiny beyond the confines of his ordinary existence. And though he could not yet comprehend the full magnitude of his calling, he felt its pull deep within his soul, urging him to seek out the truth amidst the chaos of the world around him.

The revelation filled Muhammad with a sense of awe and wonder, but it also brought with it a profound sense of responsibility. He understood that he had been chosen for a divine purpose, tasked with delivering God's message of peace, justice, and compassion to humanity.

Yet, the path ahead would not be easy. Muhammad faced staunch opposition from the powerful elites of Mecca, who viewed his message as a threat to their authority and way of life.

He endured persecution, ridicule, and even physical violence, but he remained steadfast in his commitment to his mission.

Despite the challenges he faced, Muhammad never wavered in his belief in the importance of his message. He continued to preach the message of Islam, calling upon his followers to uphold principles of equality, justice, and compassion.

Through his unwavering determination and steadfast faith, Muhammad emerged as a transformative figure in the history of humanity. His teachings laid the foundation for one of the world's major religions, and his example continues to inspire millions of people around the globe to this day.

Muhammad's early life and struggles serve as a testament to the power of resilience, compassion, and faith in the face of adversity. His journey from orphaned child to revered prophet is a reminder that even in the darkest of times, hope can endure, and a single individual can change the course of history.

Chapter 2 : Marriages of Muhammad

In the life of Prophet Muhammad, his marriages hold a significant place, reflecting various aspects of his personal life, social context, and divine guidance. Each marriage was unique, serving different purposes and providing valuable lessons for believers. Let us delve into the intricacies of these marriages, exploring their historical context, motivations, and impact.

2.1. Pre-Revelation Marriage

1. Khadijah bint Khuwaylid: Muhammad's first and most beloved wife was Khadijah bint Khuwaylid. Their union was a testament to love, respect, and partnership. Khadijah, a wealthy widow and successful businesswoman, was fifteen years older than Muhammad. Despite the age difference, their marriage was based on mutual admiration, trust, and shared values. Khadijah provided unwavering support to Muhammad, both emotionally and financially, during the early years of his prophethood. She was the first person to believe in his message and stood by his side through the trials and tribulations they faced in Mecca. Their marriage lasted for twenty-five years until Khadijah's passing, leaving a profound impact on Muhammad's life and mission.

Khadijah was no ordinary woman. She was a widow, a mother, and a successful businesswoman who commanded respect and admiration from all who knew her. Her wealth and influence were unmatched, but it was her kindness, compassion, and unwavering faith that truly set her apart.

In the heart of Mecca, Khadijah's name was synonymous with integrity and honor. Her caravan trade brought riches beyond measure, but it was her impeccable character that endeared her to the people of Mecca. She was known as "the Pure One," a title that spoke volumes about her moral fortitude and virtuous nature.

And then there was Muhammad—a man of humble beginnings, known for his honesty, kindness, and unwavering sense of justice. He was a merchant, like Khadijah, but their paths had never crossed until fate intervened in the most unexpected of ways.

It was through business dealings that Khadijah first heard of Muhammad—a young man whose reputation preceded him. Intrigued by tales of his integrity and honesty, Khadijah sought him out, eager to enlist his services for an upcoming caravan journey.

As Muhammad embarked on the journey, little did he know that it would be a journey that would change the course of his life forever. Khadijah's caravan was bound for distant lands, but it was the journey of the heart that would prove to be the most transformative.

With each passing day, Khadijah found herself drawn to Muhammad—not just for his business acumen, but for the depth of his character and the purity of his soul. She saw in him a kindred spirit, a soulmate whose presence filled her with a sense of peace and contentment she had never known before.

As their journey unfolded, so too did their love—a love that transcended boundaries of class, wealth, and societal norms. In Muhammad, Khadijah found a partner who shared her values, her dreams, and her faith. Together, they forged a bond that would withstand the test of time and endure the trials and tribulations that lay ahead.

When they returned to Mecca, Khadijah knew in her heart that she had found her soulmate in Muhammad. With courage and conviction, she approached him with a proposal that would change both their lives forever—a proposal of marriage.

For Muhammad, Khadijah's proposal was a revelation—a gift from God that filled his heart with gratitude and joy. He accepted without hesitation, knowing that in Khadijah, he had found not just a wife, but a partner, a confidante, and a pillar of strength.

Their marriage was a union of hearts, minds, and souls—a union blessed by God and celebrated by all who knew them. Together, they embarked on a journey of love, faith, and devotion—a journey that would lay the foundation for a legacy that would endure for eternity.

In Khadijah, Muhammad found not just a wife, but a source of inspiration and guidance—a woman whose unwavering faith and steadfast support would sustain him through the trials and tribulations that lay ahead. And in Muhammad, Khadijah found a husband, a friend, and a beloved companion—a man whose love and devotion would light up her life like the stars in the desert sky.

Their marriage was a testament to the power of love, faith, and devotion—a union that transcended time and space, leaving an indelible mark on the pages of history. And as they stood side by side, hand in hand, they knew that their love would endure for all eternity—a love that would inspire generations to come and illuminate the path to righteousness and truth.

Khadijah's Support to Muhammad

It was during one fateful night, as Muhammad meditated in the solitude of the Cave of Hira, that he received the first revelations of the Quran from the angel Gabriel. Overwhelmed by the magnitude of this divine encounter, Muhammad returned home to Khadijah, trembling with awe and uncertainty.

As he recounted the events of that night to Khadijah, her heart swelled with pride and reverence. She knew in her soul that Muhammad was destined for greatness, chosen by God to deliver His message to humanity. With unwavering faith and conviction, Khadijah embraced Muhammad's revelation, offering him her unconditional support and encouragement.

Together, Khadijah and Muhammad embarked on a journey of faith and transformation—a journey that would forever alter the course of history. With Khadijah by his side, Muhammad found the strength and courage to face the challenges that lay ahead, knowing that he was not alone in his mission.

Khadijah's unwavering faith and steadfast support were a source of comfort and inspiration to Muhammad as he navigated the trials and tribulations of his prophetic mission. She stood by him through every trial and hardship, offering him her wisdom, her strength, and her unwavering love.

In Khadijah, Muhammad found not just a wife, but a true partner in faith—a woman whose faith in God mirrored his own, whose devotion to Islam was unwavering, and whose love for him was boundless. And in Muhammad, Khadijah found a messenger of God—a man whose words would echo through the ages, whose teachings would transform hearts and minds, and whose legacy would endure for all eternity.

2.2. Post-Revelation Marriages

1. Sawda bint Zam'a: After the death of Khadijah, Muhammad married Sawda bint Zam'a, a widow who had migrated to Abyssinia (modern-day Ethiopia) with her husband during the early persecution of Muslims in Mecca. Sawda was known for her piety, kindness, and devotion to Islam. Muhammad's marriage to Sawda provided her with protection and support, as she had been left vulnerable after the death of her husband. Their marriage was a testament to Muhammad's compassion and concern for the welfare of widows in society.

2. Aisha bint Abu Bakr: Aisha bint Abu Bakr, the daughter of Muhammad's close companion Abu Bakr, was betrothed to Muhammad at a young age and married him when she was around nine years old. Aisha played a significant role in the development of Islam, as she was known for her sharp intellect, knowledge of Islamic jurisprudence, and narrations of Hadith (sayings and actions of Prophet Muhammad). Her marriage to Muhammad strengthened the bond between Muhammad and Abu Bakr, further solidifying the unity of the early Muslim community. Despite controversy surrounding her age at the time of marriage, Aisha's relationship with Muhammad was marked by love, respect, and companionship.

3. Hafsa bint Umar: Hafsa bint Umar, the daughter of the second caliph Umar ibn al-Khattab, became one of Muhammad's wives after her previous marriage ended in divorce. Hafsa was known for her piety and dedication to Islam. Her marriage to Muhammad strengthened the ties between Muhammad and Umar, fostering greater unity within the

Muslim community. Hafsa's role as one of the "Mothers of the Believers" (Ummahat al-Mu'minin) symbolized her status as a respected and honored member of the Muslim community.

4. Zaynab bint Khuzayma: Zaynab bint Khuzayma, also known as Umm al-Masakin (Mother of the Poor), was a widow known for her charitable deeds and generosity. Muhammad married Zaynab after the Battle of Badr, during a time when many Muslim men had been martyred, leaving behind widows and orphans in need of support. Zaynab's marriage to Muhammad provided her with protection and security, while also highlighting the importance of caring for the vulnerable members of society.

5. Umm Salama Hind bint Abi Umayya: Umm Salama Hind bint Abi Umayya was a widow with children who had immigrated to Medina with her husband. After her husband's death, Umm Salama faced challenges and uncertainty about her future. Muhammad's marriage to Umm Salama provided her with stability, protection, and companionship. Umm Salama's wisdom, piety, and devotion to Islam made her a respected figure in the Muslim community, and her marriage to Muhammad strengthened her position as one of the "Mothers of the Believers."

6. Zaynab bint Jahsh: Zaynab bint Jahsh was Muhammad's cousin and the wife of his adopted son Zayd ibn Harithah. Their marriage was unconventional, as Zaynab had initially rejected Muhammad's proposal due to social norms and familial ties. However, after receiving divine revelation affirming the legitimacy of the marriage, Muhammad married Zaynab, breaking cultural taboos and setting an example of equality and justice. Zaynab's marriage to Muhammad served as a powerful testament to the abolishment of societal hierarchies and the importance of following divine guidance.

7. Juwayriya bint al-Harith: Juwayriya bint al -Harith was from the Banu Mustaliq tribe, which had been defeated by the Muslims in battle. As part of the spoils of war, Juwayriya was among the captives taken by the Muslims. Muhammad married Juwayriya, not only to grant her freedom and dignity but also to strengthen the bonds of kinship and unity between the Muslim community and the defeated tribe. Juwayriya's marriage to Muhammad symbolized the transformative power of compassion and forgiveness in building bridges between communities.

8. **Umm Habiba Ramla bint Abi Sufyan:** Umm Habiba Ramla bint Abi Sufyan was the daughter of Abu Sufyan, a prominent leader of the Quraysh tribe and a staunch opponent of Islam. Despite her father's opposition, Umm Habiba embraced Islam and immigrated to Abyssinia (modern-day Ethiopia) with her husband, who later apostatized and abandoned her. Muhammad proposed marriage to Umm Habiba, offering her protection and support in her time of need. Umm Habiba's marriage to Muhammad symbolized her unwavering faith and commitment to Islam, despite facing personal challenges and familial opposition.

9. **Maymunah bint al-Harith:** Maymunah bint al-Harith was a widow who had been previously married to Muhammad's cousin. Muhammad married Maymunah during his pilgrimage to Mecca, strengthening the ties between the Muslim community and the Quraysh tribe. Maymunah's marriage to

Muhammad provided her with security and protection, while also highlighting the importance of fostering alliances and reconciliation within society.

Conclusion:

Muhammad's marriages were not merely personal affairs but carried significant social, political, and religious implications. Each marriage served a unique purpose, whether it was to provide protection and support to widows, strengthen alliances between tribes, or uphold the principles of justice and equality. Through his marriages, Muhammad set an example of compassion, empathy, and inclusivity, demonstrating the transformative power of love and unity in building a harmonious society.

Chapter 3 : The Calling

In the bustling streets of Mecca, where the sun beat down upon the sandstone walls and the scent of spices lingered in the air, Muhammad faced and experienced a lot from his life and surrondings. He walked among the throngs of merchants and pilgrims with a quiet dignity, his presence commanding respect from all who crossed his path. Known for his honesty, kindness, and unwavering sense of justice, Muhammad was a pillar of his community—a man whose integrity shone like a beacon in the midst of chaos.

Yet, despite the outward tranquility of his life, Muhammad felt a stirring within him—a calling that whispered of something greater, something beyond the mundane routines of everyday existence. It was a feeling that tugged at his soul, urging him to seek out the truth amidst the clamor of the world around him.

In moments of reflection, Muhammad sought solace in the quiet solitude of the desert, where the shifting sands and endless horizon seemed to stretch on for eternity. Amidst the vast expanse of the desert, there was a particular sanctuary that drew him in—the Cave of Hira. Nestled within the rugged mountains near Mecca, this cave offered Muhammad a refuge from the distractions of the bustling city below. Here, amidst the rocky walls and serene surroundings, he could immerse himself in prayer, contemplation, and communion with the divine. It was in the hushed confines of the Cave of Hira that Muhammad found the clarity and spiritual connection he sought, paving the way for the profound revelations that would shape the course of history.

It was there, he felt the presence of something divine—a force that transcended the boundaries of mortal understanding.

As he gazed up at the twinkling stars, their light shimmering like diamonds against the velvet canvas of the night, Muhammad felt a sense of awe wash over him. It was in those moments of contemplation that he heard it—the gentle voice that seemed to echo in the depths of his being, guiding him towards a path of righteousness and compassion.

It was as if the very heavens themselves were reaching out to him, calling him to a higher purpose—a purpose that transcended the mundane concerns of everyday life. And in the midst of that divine symphony, Muhammad heard it—the gentle voice that seemed to echo in the depths of his being, resonating with the wisdom of the ages.

"O Muhammad," the voice whispered, its melody like the sweetest music to his ears, "you have been chosen for a great task—a task that will test your resolve, challenge your beliefs, and lead you down a path of righteousness and compassion."

Each word echoed in Muhammad's heart, resonating with a weight and significance that seemed to reverberate through his very soul. As the ethereal voice spoke, its message carried a gravity that left him breathless, as if the very fabric of the universe had shifted to accommodate its divine decree.

In that moment, Muhammad felt as though he stood on the threshold of an existence far grander than anything he had ever imagined—a reality where the boundaries of time and space blurred, and the mundane concerns of everyday life paled in comparison to the magnitude of his calling.

With each passing moment, the voice grew stronger, its message ringing clear in Muhammad's heart. It spoke of justice for the oppressed, mercy for the downtrodden, and love for all of God's creation. It spoke of a world where the bonds of brotherhood transcended the barriers of race, religion, and nationality—a world where peace reigned supreme and all were equal in the eyes of their Creator.

The realization washed over him like a tidal wave, flooding his senses with a potent mix of awe and trepidation. He knew, with a certainty that bordered on instinct, that he was being summoned to a destiny beyond the confines of his ordinary life—a destiny that would demand everything he had to give and more.

The weight of the revelation settled upon him like a heavy cloak, pressing down upon his shoulders with an almost tangible force. Yet, despite the enormity of the task ahead, Muhammad felt a stirring of excitement deep within his soul—a sense of purpose that burned bright amidst the darkness of uncertainty.

For he knew that he had been chosen not by chance or happenstance, but by the hand of God Himself—a realization that filled him with a profound sense of humility and awe. And it was with that knowledge that he accepted his divine calling, knowing that he was being called to a purpose far greater than himself.

With each passing moment, the gravity of his decision became ever more apparent, as the magnitude of his mission began to dawn upon him in all its splendor. He understood that he was being called to lead his people out of the darkness of ignorance and into the light of truth—to be a beacon of hope in a world beset by chaos and confusion.

And though the road ahead would be fraught with peril and uncertainty, Muhammad faced it with a courage born of faith and a resolve forged in the fires of divine inspiration. For he knew that he was not alone—that God's hand would guide him through even the darkest of nights, illuminating the path before him with the light of His infinite wisdom and grace.

And so, with a heart full of hope and a spirit ablaze with purpose, Muhammad embarked on the greatest journey of his life—a journey that would leave an indelible mark on the world and inspire countless generations to come.

Trembling with awe and wonder, Muhammad bowed his head in reverence, his heart overflowing with gratitude for the divine guidance that had been bestowed upon him. For in that moment, amidst the stillness of the desert night, he knew that his life would never be the same—that he had been called to a destiny far greater than he could ever have imagined.

And so, with a heart full of hope and a spirit ablaze with divine inspiration, Muhammad embraced his calling wholeheartedly, knowing that the journey ahead would be long and arduous, but also filled with moments of profound revelation and divine grace.

In the days and weeks that followed, Muhammad delved deeper into the teachings of his faith, seeking guidance and inspiration from the words of the prophets who had come before him. With each passing moment, his conviction grew stronger, until he could no longer ignore the voice that beckoned him towards a destiny beyond his wildest dreams.

And so, with a sense of purpose burning brightly within him, Muhammad embraced his calling wholeheartedly, knowing that the journey ahead would be filled with challenges and obstacles, but also with moments of profound revelation and divine grace.

For in the heart of every believer, there lies a calling—a whisper from the heavens that reminds us of our true purpose in this world. And it is in answering that call, with courage and conviction, that we discover the true meaning of our existence, and the boundless depths of love and compassion that lie within us all.

Chapter 4 : The Revelation

In the serene solitude of the Cave of Hira, Muhammad first felt the presence of the divine. As he sought solace in prayer and contemplation, he was suddenly overcome by a radiant light that seemed to illuminate the very depths of his soul.

In that moment, an ethereal figure appeared before him—a being of celestial beauty and grace. It was the Angel Gabriel, messenger of God, whose presence filled the cave with a sense of peace and majesty. With gentle yet commanding words, Gabriel conveyed to Muhammad the first verses of revelation, setting in motion a divine encounter that would change the course of history.

Though the details of how Gabriel convinced Muhammad may vary in different accounts, one thing remained constant—the overwhelming sense of spiritual presence and guidance that permeated the cave. Through words of reassurance, wisdom, and divine revelation, Gabriel instilled in Muhammad a sense of purpose and mission, reassuring him of his chosen role as the Messenger of God. And as Muhammad beheld the radiant presence of the angel before him, he knew in his heart that he was destined for greatness—that he was chosen to carry forth a message of truth, compassion, and guidance for all humanity.

While the details of how Gabriel convinced Muhammad may vary in different accounts, there are several key aspects that are commonly emphasized:

1. Presence and Majesty: When the angel Gabriel appeared to Muhammad, his presence was awe-inspiring and majestic.

Gabriel's appearance radiated with divine light, filling the cave with an otherworldly glow. The sheer magnitude of Gabriel's presence conveyed a sense of authority and importance, immediately capturing Muhammad's attention and reverence.

2. Direct Command: Gabriel delivered a direct command to Muhammad, instructing him to "Read" or "Recite" in the name of his Lord. This command was not a mere suggestion but a divine imperative, compelling Muhammad to listen and obey. The clarity and urgency of Gabriel's command left no room for doubt or hesitation, prompting Muhammad to heed the angel's words.

3. Revelation of Verses: Gabriel conveyed the first verses of revelation to Muhammad, revealing the words of God that would become the foundation of Islam. These verses were profound and powerful, resonating deeply with Muhammad's heart and soul. Through the revelation of these verses, Gabriel provided Muhammad with tangible evidence of his divine mission, convincing him of the truth and authenticity of his calling.

Over a time, with each revelation, Muhammad's heart swelled with love for humanity, and his mission became clear—to guide his people towards the light of truth and righteousness.

4. Divine Guidance and Assurance: Throughout the encounter, Gabriel offered Muhammad divine guidance and assurance, reassuring him of God's presence and support. Gabriel's words conveyed a sense of comfort and reassurance, alleviating any fears or doubts that Muhammad may have had. By reaffirming God's guidance and protection, Gabriel instilled

in Muhammad the confidence and resolve to embrace his role as the messenger of God.

Overall, Gabriel's encounter with Muhammad in the Cave of Hira was a transformative experience that convinced Muhammad of the truth and importance of his divine mission. Through his presence, command, revelation of verses, and assurance of divine guidance, Gabriel played a crucial role in convincing Muhammad to accept his calling and embark on the journey of prophethood.

Chapter 5: Sharing his Revelation

In the wake of his profound encounter with the Angel Gabriel in the Cave of Hira, Muhammad found himself entrusted with a sacred mission—to spread the message of divine revelation to the people of Mecca and beyond. With a heart ablaze with the fire of divine guidance and a soul stirred by the call to righteousness, Muhammad embarked on a journey that would forever alter the course of history.

At first, Muhammad grappled with the weight of his newfound responsibility. The magnitude of the revelation he had received filled him with awe and trepidation, and he wondered how he could possibly convey such profound truths to a world steeped in ignorance and disbelief. Yet, guided by the wisdom and reassurance of the Angel Gabriel, Muhammad found the courage to step forth into the world and proclaim the message entrusted to him.

With unwavering faith and conviction, Muhammad began to share the revelations he had received with those closest to him—his family, his friends, and his fellow tribesmen. He spoke of the oneness of God, the importance of faith and submission, and the need for justice, compassion, and righteousness in all aspects of life. Though met with skepticism and resistance from some quarters, Muhammad's words resonated deeply with those who were receptive to the truth.

His approach to sharing his revelations with others evolved over time as he navigated the complexities of spreading his message in a society resistant to change. Here's how Muhammad began to talk about his revelations to the people:

1. Private Sharing with Close Family and Friends: Initially, Muhammad shared his revelations in private settings with his closest family members and friends. He began by confiding in his wife, Khadijah, who was his steadfast supporter and confidante. He also shared his experiences with his close friends and companions, such as Abu Bakr, Ali ibn Abi Talib, and Zaid ibn Harithah. These private discussions allowed Muhammad to test the waters and gauge the reactions of those closest to him before sharing his message more broadly.

2. Gradual Revelation to the Public: As Muhammad gained confidence in his role as a prophet and messenger of God, he began to share his revelations with a wider audience. He started by preaching to small gatherings of people in Mecca, including family members, friends, and curious onlookers. Over time, as his following grew, Muhammad expanded his audience to include members of the wider Meccan community, including tribespeople, merchants, and travelers passing through the city.

3. Use of Oral Communication and Recitation: Muhammad primarily conveyed his revelations orally, reciting the verses of the Quran to his listeners. His eloquence and sincerity captivated his audience, drawing them in with the beauty and power of his words. Muhammad's recitations were often accompanied by explanations and interpretations, providing context and guidance for understanding the divine message.

4. Appeal to Monotheism and Moral Principles: In his public preaching, Muhammad emphasized the central tenets of Islam, including monotheism (belief in the oneness of God) and moral principles such as justice, compassion, and social responsibility. He called upon his listeners to abandon idolatry and embrace the worship of the one true God, urging them to uphold ethical values and treat one another with kindness and respect.

5. Challenges and Opposition: Muhammad faced significant challenges and opposition from the Meccan elite, who viewed his message as a threat to their power and influence. Despite facing persecution, ridicule, and even physical violence, Muhammad remained steadfast in his commitment to spreading the message of Islam. He continued to preach with courage and determination, undeterred by the obstacles in his path.

As word of Muhammad's teachings spread throughout Mecca, so too did opposition and hostility from the Quraysh community, the powerful tribe that ruled the city. Muhammad faced ridicule, persecution, and even threats to his life as he continued to proclaim the message of divine revelation with unwavering determination and courage.

Undeterred by adversity, Muhammad sought out opportunities to engage with people from all walks of life, sharing the message of Islam with sincerity, compassion, and patience. He engaged in dialogue with the leaders of Mecca, seeking to win their hearts and minds with the power of his words and the purity of his character. He reached out to the marginalized and downtrodden, offering them hope, dignity, and a sense of belonging in the community of believers.

Muhammad's message transcended the confines of tribalism, ethnicity, and social status, inviting all humanity to embrace the path of truth and righteousness. His teachings resonated with people's hearts and souls, touching the deepest recesses of their being and inspiring them to seek a higher purpose in life.

However, the effort and success of Muhammad was intolerable to manies including The Quraysh community. They intensified their efforts to suppress the spread of Islam, resorting to persecution, economic boycotts, and even physical violence in their attempts to silence Muhammad and his followers. Yet, in the face of adversity, Muhammad remained steadfast in his commitment to the message of divine revelation, drawing strength from his unwavering faith in God and the support of his devoted companions.

His tireless efforts to convey the message of Islam laid the foundation for a global faith community that would endure for centuries to come, inspiring countless generations to embrace the teachings of peace, justice, and compassion that he so passionately championed.

Overall, Muhammad's approach to sharing his revelations with the people of Mecca was characterized by gradualism, patience, and perseverance. Through his engaging oral communication, appeal to monotheism and moral principles, and unwavering commitment to his mission, Muhammad succeeded in attracting a following and laying the foundation for the spread of Islam.

Chapter 6: Trials and Tribulations

As the message of Islam began to spread throughout Mecca, Muhammad found himself facing mounting opposition from the powerful elites of the city. Threatened by his message of equality, justice, and monotheism, they sought to undermine his authority and suppress his teachings through various means of persecution and harassment.

Despite the growing hostility against him, Muhammad remained firm in his mission, drawing strength from his unwavering faith in God and the unwavering support of his devoted companions. With each passing day, the trials and tribulations he faced only served to deepen his resolve and commitment to spreading the message of Islam.

The powers of Mecca, led by the Quraysh tribe, unleashed a campaign of persecution against Muhammad and his followers. They subjected them to ridicule, mockery, and social ostracization, seeking to discredit and marginalize them in the eyes of the community. Muhammad himself became the target of slander and false accusations, as his adversaries sought to undermine his credibility and tarnish his reputation.

Yet, despite the relentless persecution, Muhammad refused to be silenced. He continued to preach the message of Islam with courage and conviction, undeterred by the obstacles in his path. His unwavering faith in God and his unshakeable belief in the truth of his message sustained him through even the darkest of times.

One of the earliest and most insidious forms of opposition Muhammad encountered came in the form of slander and defamation propagated by his enemies. The Quraysh, alarmed by the growing influence of Islam and threatened by Muhammad's calls for social justice and equality, launched a smear campaign aimed at tarnishing his reputation and discrediting his message. False accusations of sorcery, poetry, and madness were leveled against Muhammad in an attempt to sow doubt and suspicion among his followers and dissuade others from embracing his teachings.

In addition, Muhammad faced physical threats and acts of violence from those opposed to his message. The Quraysh and other tribes allied with them sought to suppress the spread of Islam through intimidation, harassment, and outright aggression. Muhammad and his followers endured persecution, boycotts, and even assassination attempts as they steadfastly adhered to their faith and principles.

One of the most harrowing examples of this persecution is the story of Sumayyah bint Khayyat, one of the earliest converts to Islam and the first martyr in Islamic history. Sumayyah, along with her husband Yasir and their son Ammar, faced relentless torture and persecution at the hands of the Quraysh for their refusal to renounce their faith. Despite enduring unimaginable suffering, Sumayyah remained steadfast in her belief in Allah and Muhammad as His messenger, becoming a symbol of resilience and steadfastness in the face of adversity.

Another example of the Quraysh's efforts to thwart Muhammad's mission is the economic boycott imposed on Muhammad and his followers, known as the "Boycott of Banu Hashim." The Quraysh, seeking to isolate and weaken Muhammad's supporters, imposed a social and economic embargo on the Banu Hashim clan, cutting off their access to food, trade, and other essential resources. The boycott lasted for three years and inflicted immense hardship on Muhammad and his followers, yet they remained steadfast in their faith and resilience, refusing to abandon their beliefs despite the immense pressure.

Despite the myriad challenges and obstacles he faced, Muhammad remained resolute in his mission, drawing strength from his unwavering faith in God and the support of his devoted companions. His steadfastness in the face of adversity inspired countless generations to come, serving as a testament to the transformative power of faith, perseverance, and resilience in the face of oppression and injustice.

Throughout this period of trial and tribulation, Muhammad found solace and strength in the companionship of his devoted followers. They stood by his side through thick and thin, offering him unwavering support and solidarity in the face of adversity. Their loyalty and dedication bolstered Muhammad's spirits and reaffirmed his conviction that he was indeed on the right path.

As the persecution intensified, Muhammad and his followers faced increasing threats to their safety and well-being. Some were subjected to physical violence and torture, while others endured economic hardship and social marginalization. Yet, through it all, they remained steadfast in their faith, refusing to renounce their beliefs or compromise their principles.

In the face of such trials and tribulations, Muhammad's resilience and perseverance shone brightly, serving as an inspiration to all who witnessed his steadfastness. His unwavering commitment to his mission, despite the immense challenges he faced, was a testament to the strength of his character and the depth of his faith in God.

As the dark clouds of persecution loomed overhead, Muhammad remained undaunted, knowing that he was guided by a higher purpose and protected by the divine hand of God. With each trial and tribulation he faced, his resolve only grew stronger, as he continued to spread the message of Islam with unwavering determination and unwavering hope for a better tomorrow.

Chapter 7: The Hijrah

Amidst the escalating persecution in Mecca, Muhammad and his followers faced mounting threats to their safety and well-being. In the face of this adversity, they made the momentous decision to embark on a perilous journey to the city of Medina—a journey that would come to be known as the Hijrah.

The Hijrah marked a pivotal moment in Islamic history, symbolizing the triumph of faith over adversity and the resilience of the Muslim community in the face of persecution. For Muhammad and his followers, it represented a leap of faith into the unknown, as they left behind their homes, families, and possessions in pursuit of religious freedom and sanctuary.

As Muhammad and his companions made their way to Medina, they encountered numerous challenges and dangers along the way. They faced harsh conditions, treacherous terrain, and the constant threat of pursuit by their enemies. Yet, despite the hardships they endured, their spirits remained undaunted, fueled by their unwavering faith in God and their commitment to the teachings of Islam.

Upon reaching Medina, Muhammad and his followers found sanctuary among a community eager to embrace their teachings. The people of Medina welcomed them with open arms, offering them shelter, support, and protection from their enemies in Mecca. It was here, amidst the fertile oasis of Medina, that Muhammad and his companions would lay the foundations of a new society—a society built upon the principles of justice, compassion, and brotherhood.

In Medina, Muhammad's message found fertile ground, resonating deeply with the hearts and minds of the people. His teachings of monotheism, social justice, and moral integrity struck a chord with the residents of the city, drawing them into the fold of Islam in ever-increasing numbers. From merchants to farmers, from tribal leaders to slaves, people from all walks of life embraced Islam, united by their shared faith and commitment to building a better future.

Despite the challenges they faced in establishing themselves in a new city, Muhammad and his followers remained firm in their determination to spread the message of Islam. Through their collective efforts, they transformed Medina into a model community—a shining example of what could be achieved when people came together in pursuit of a common goal.

The Hijrah was not merely a physical journey from one place to another; it was a spiritual and moral journey that transformed the lives of all who undertook it. It was a testament to the power of faith, perseverance, and unity in the face of adversity—a legacy that continues to inspire Muslims around the world to this day.

Fights between Muhammad and Oppositions

It was in the crucible of Medina that Muhammad's physical struggles with his adversaries reached a critical juncture. The Battle of Badr, fought in the second year of the Hijrah, marked the first armed confrontation between the Muslims and the Quraysh. Despite being vastly outnumbered and ill-equipped, Muhammad and his followers emerged victorious, securing a decisive victory that bolstered their morale and strengthened their resolve.

Yet, the Battle of Badr was only the beginning of Muhammad's military campaigns against the Quraysh and other adversaries. Over the course of his prophetic mission, Muhammad engaged in a series of battles and skirmishes aimed at defending the fledgling Muslim community from external threats and ensuring the survival and propagation of Islam. These included the battles of Uhud, Khandaq, and Hunayn, among others, each of which tested Muhammad's leadership, strategic acumen, and martial prowess.

Muhammad's physical struggles with his adversaries were not undertaken out of a thirst for power or conquest, but out of necessity to defend the nascent Muslim community from existential threats and ensure the survival of Islam. Despite the challenges and sacrifices he endured, Muhammad remained steadfast in his commitment to his mission, guided by the principles of justice, compassion, and righteousness that defined his prophetic message. His physical struggles serve as a testament to his unwavering faith, courage, and determination in the face of adversity, inspiring generations to come with his example of resilience and fortitude in the pursuit of truth and justice.

Chapter 8 : The Battles

In the tumultuous landscape of 7th-century Arabia, Prophet Muhammad faced a series of military confrontations known as battles, each arising out of unique circumstances and challenges that tested the resolve and faith of the early Muslim community. These battles were not waged out of a thirst for power or conquest, but rather as defensive measures aimed at protecting the fledgling Muslim community from external threats and ensuring the survival and propagation of Islam in the face of relentless opposition and hostility.

The first major battle fought by Muhammad and his followers was the Battle of Badr, which took place in the second year of the Hijrah (migration) to Medina. Born out of the Quraysh tribe's relentless persecution and hostility towards the Muslim community, the Battle of Badr was a defensive action aimed at intercepting a Quraysh caravan returning from Syria and securing much-needed resources for the Muslim community. Despite being vastly outnumbered and ill-equipped, the Muslim army under the leadership of Muhammad emerged victorious, securing a decisive triumph that bolstered the morale of the Muslim community and affirmed Muhammad's status as the chosen messenger of God.

Following the Battle of Badr, Muhammad and his followers faced continued threats and aggression from their adversaries, culminating in a series of military confrontations aimed at defending the Muslim community and safeguarding the integrity of Islam. The Battle of Uhud, fought the following year, saw the Muslim army suffer a temporary setback due to a lapse in discipline and strategic oversight, yet Muhammad's leadership and steadfastness ultimately ensured that the Muslims retained control of Medina and repelled the Quraysh onslaught.

The Battle of the Trench, also known as the Battle of Khandaq, was another pivotal engagement that tested the resolve and ingenuity of the Muslim community. Faced with a formidable coalition of tribes intent on annihilating the Muslims once and for all, Muhammad and his followers devised a defensive strategy that involved digging a trench around the city of Medina to thwart the enemy's advance. Through their unity, resourcefulness, and unwavering faith, the Muslims successfully repelled the coalition forces, securing a hard-won victory that safeguarded the future of Islam in Arabia.

In addition to these major battles, Muhammad and his followers engaged in a series of smaller skirmishes and expeditions aimed at defending the Muslim community from external threats and expanding the boundaries of Islam. These included the expeditions of Banu Qurayzah, Banu Nadir, and Banu Mustaliq, among others, each of which served to consolidate the authority of Muhammad and establish Islam as a dominant force in the region.

Throughout these battles and expeditions, Muhammad's leadership and strategic acumen were instrumental in guiding the Muslim community through times of adversity and ensuring the survival and propagation of Islam. His unwavering faith in God, coupled with his dedication to justice, compassion, and righteousness, inspired his followers to persevere in the face of seemingly insurmountable odds and remain steadfast in their commitment to the cause of Islam.

Ultimately, the battles fought by Muhammad were not mere military campaigns, but rather spiritual and ideological struggles aimed at upholding the principles of truth, justice, and righteousness in the face of oppression and tyranny. Through their sacrifices and perseverance, Muhammad and his followers laid the foundation for a global faith community that continues to draw inspiration from their example of courage, resilience, and unwavering devotion to the cause of Islam.

Let's discuss some major Battles of his time that remind for the victory of trueness, strength, faith, firmness and righteousness.

8.1 Battle of Badr

In the annals of Islamic history, few events loom as large as the Battle of Badr—a momentous clash that would come to define the early years of Prophet Muhammad's mission and shape the course of Islam for generations to come. Born out of the crucible of adversity and uncertainty, the Battle of Badr stands as a testament to the resilience, faith, and unwavering determination of the early Muslim community in the face of overwhelming odds.

The backdrop to the Battle of Badr was a period of intense persecution and hostility faced by the Muslims at the hands of the Quraysh tribe in Mecca. Prophet Muhammad and his followers had endured years of harassment, persecution, and even attempts on their lives as they sought to peacefully propagate the message of Islam. Faced with mounting oppression and threats to their safety, Muhammad and his companions made the fateful decision to seek refuge in the neighboring city of Medina—a move that would set the stage for the momentous events to come.

Yet, even in Medina, the Muslim community found little respite from the relentless hostility of their adversaries. The Quraysh, alarmed by the growing influence of Islam and determined to crush the fledgling Muslim community, marshaled their forces for a decisive confrontation with Muhammad and his followers. Led by their leaders, Abu Jahl and Abu Sufyan, the Quraysh assembled a formidable army of well-equipped warriors, intent on eradicating the perceived threat posed by Islam once and for all.

It was against this backdrop of imminent danger and uncertainty that the Battle of Badr unfolded. In the month of Ramadan, in the second year of the Hijrah, the Muslim community received intelligence of a Quraysh caravan returning from Syria laden with goods and wealth. Seeing an opportunity to intercept the caravan and alleviate the economic hardships faced by his followers, Muhammad mobilized a small band of 313 men and set out towards Badr—a strategic location along the caravan's route.

The Battle of Badr was fought on the plains of Badr, a barren expanse of desert located approximately 80 miles southwest of Medina. Despite being vastly outnumbered and ill-equipped, the Muslim army under the leadership of Muhammad displayed remarkable courage, discipline, and strategic acumen. Utilizing the terrain to their advantage, Muhammad devised a plan that allowed his forces to effectively neutralize the numerical superiority of the Quraysh and inflict significant casualties upon their ranks.

As the battle raged on, the tide of fortune shifted in favor of the Muslims, bolstered by their unwavering faith in God and their trust in the leadership of Muhammad. Against all odds, the Muslim army emerged victorious, dealing a crushing blow to the Quraysh and securing a decisive triumph that would reverberate throughout the Arabian Peninsula.

The Battle of Badr was not merely a military victory; it was a triumph of faith, resilience, and divine providence. For the Muslim community, it served as a powerful validation of their beliefs and a testament to the transformative power of unwavering faith in the face of adversity. For Prophet Muhammad, it marked a pivotal moment in his prophetic mission, affirming his status as the chosen messenger of God and laying the foundation for the eventual triumph of Islam over ignorance and oppression.

The Battle of Badr stands as a timeless testament to the enduring legacy of courage, sacrifice, and faith that defines the early Muslim community and continues to inspire believers around the world today. It serves as a reminder that, even in the darkest of times, the power of faith and perseverance can overcome seemingly insurmountable obstacles and pave the way for a brighter future filled with hope and promise.

8.2 Battle of Uhud

Born out of a complex web of tribal rivalries, political intrigue, and religious fervor, the Battle of Uhud was a turning point in the struggle between the fledgling Muslim community led by Prophet Muhammad and the Quraysh tribe of Mecca, determined to crush the growing influence of Islam once and for all.

The roots of the Battle of Uhud can be traced back to the aftermath of the Battle of Badr, where the Muslims achieved a remarkable victory against the Quraysh, despite being vastly outnumbered. Smarting from their defeat and eager for revenge, the Quraysh began to marshal their forces for a decisive confrontation with Muhammad and his followers, gathering a formidable army of well-equipped warriors intent on eradicating the perceived threat posed by Islam.

Faced with the looming threat of a Quraysh invasion, Muhammad and his companions made the fateful decision to confront their adversaries head-on, marshaling a force of approximately 1,000 men to defend the city of Medina and protect the fledgling Muslim community from external aggression. The stage was set for a showdown that would test the mettle of the Muslim community and the leadership of its Prophet.

As the two armies converged on the battlefield of Uhud, located approximately 4 miles north of Medina, Muhammad and his followers braced themselves for the impending clash. The Muslim army, though outnumbered, was bolstered by its unwavering faith in God and its trust in the leadership of

Muhammad, who devised a strategic plan aimed at neutralizing the numerical superiority of the Quraysh and securing victory for the Muslims.

However, despite Muhammad's careful planning and the initial success of the Muslim forces, the Battle of Uhud took a dramatic turn when a contingent of Muslim archers disobeyed Muhammad's orders and abandoned their positions on the slopes of the Uhud mountain in pursuit of enemy spoils. This critical lapse in discipline allowed the Quraysh cavalry to exploit a gap in the Muslim defense and launch a devastating counterattack, causing confusion and disarray among the ranks of the Muslim army.

In the midst of the chaos and confusion, Muhammad himself was wounded, sustaining injuries to his face and head. Despite the pain and hardship he endured, Muhammad remained steadfast in his resolve, rallying his companions and urging them to stand firm in the face of adversity. With his leadership and guidance, the Muslim forces managed to regroup and repel the Quraysh onslaught, preventing the total collapse of their defenses and securing a semblance of victory in the aftermath of the battle.

Yet, the Battle of Uhud would ultimately end in a stalemate, with neither side able to claim a decisive triumph. While the Muslims had managed to repel the Quraysh assault and retain control of Medina, they had suffered significant casualties, including the loss of some of their most prominent companions. Despite the setbacks and hardships they faced, Muhammad and his followers emerged from the Battle of Uhud with their faith and determination intact, strengthened by their unwavering commitment to the cause of Islam and their trust in the guidance of their Prophet.

8.3 Battle of Khandaq

Battle of Khandaq, also known as the Battle of the Trench. Born out of a precarious moment in the fledgling Muslim community's history, the Battle of Khandaq would come to epitomize the strategic prowess and unwavering determination of Prophet Muhammad and his companions in the face of overwhelming odds and imminent danger.

The Battle of Khandaq was sparked by a coalition of tribes from Mecca, led by the Quraysh, who sought to crush the burgeoning Muslim community once and for all. Faced with mounting opposition and hostility from their adversaries, Muhammad and his followers in Medina found themselves besieged on all sides, their very survival hanging in the balance. In response to the growing threat, Muhammad devised a bold defensive strategy aimed at thwarting the enemy's advance and safeguarding the city of Medina from invasion.

Central to Muhammad's plan was the construction of a trench, or khandaq, around the vulnerable outskirts of Medina—a formidable barrier designed to deter the enemy's cavalry and prevent a direct assault on the city. With the help of his companions, Muhammad oversaw the excavation of the trench, rallying the Muslim community to work tirelessly in defense of their homeland and their faith.

As the coalition forces approached the city of Medina, they were met with the formidable obstacle of the trench—a seemingly insurmountable barrier that forced them to rethink their strategy and tactics. Unable to breach the defenses of the Muslim city, the Quraysh and their allies found themselves frustrated and demoralized, their plans for conquest thwarted by the sheer determination and resourcefulness of Muhammad and his companions.

Despite their numerical superiority and superior weaponry, the coalition forces were unable to overcome the defenses of the Muslim city, and after several days of stalemate, they were forced to retreat in defeat. The Battle of Khandaq thus ended in a decisive victory for the Muslims, who emerged from the conflict emboldened and strengthened in their faith and their commitment to the cause of Islam.

The Battle of Khandaq was not merely a military triumph; it was a triumph of faith, resilience, and divine providence. For the Muslim community, it served as a powerful testament to the power of unity, determination, and unwavering faith in the face of adversity. For Prophet Muhammad, it was a demonstration of his leadership and strategic acumen, reaffirming his status as the chosen messenger of God and the protector of his people.

The Battle of Khandaq stands as a timeless reminder of the enduring legacy of courage, sacrifice, and faith that defines the early Muslim community and continues to inspire believers around the world today. It serves as a testament to the transformative power of faith and perseverance in the face of seemingly insurmountable odds, and a powerful testament to the enduring legacy of Prophet Muhammad and his companions in the annals of Islamic history.

8.4 Conquest of Mecca

In the annals of Islamic history, few events hold as much significance as the Battle and Conquest of Mecca—a momentous turning point that marked the culmination of Prophet Muhammad's prophetic mission and the triumph of Islam over the forces of ignorance and oppression. Born out of years of persecution, hostility, and exile, the conquest of Mecca stands as a testament to the unwavering faith, perseverance, and strategic acumen of Muhammad and his companions in the face of seemingly insurmountable odds.

The Battle and Conquest of Mecca was sparked by the growing tensions between the Muslim community in Medina and the Quraysh tribe of Mecca, who had long been hostile towards Muhammad and his followers. Faced with relentless persecution and attempts on their lives, Muhammad and his companions sought refuge in Medina, where they built a thriving community and continued to spread the message of Islam.

Despite their exile from Mecca, Muhammad and his companions never lost sight of their ultimate goal—the liberation of their homeland from the grip of ignorance and tyranny. As the Muslim community in Medina grew in strength and numbers, Muhammad began to lay the groundwork for the eventual conquest of Mecca, forging alliances with neighboring tribes and marshaling his forces for the inevitable showdown with his adversaries.

The conquest of Mecca began with a daring and strategic maneuver known as the Treaty of Hudaybiyyah, in which

Muhammad negotiated a truce with the Quraysh that allowed the Muslims to visit the Kaaba—a sacred sanctuary in Mecca—without fear of reprisal. This temporary peace allowed Muhammad to consolidate his forces and prepare for the decisive moment that would come to define the future of Islam in Arabia.

In the eighth year of the Hijrah, Muhammad and his followers set out from Medina towards Mecca, their hearts filled with hope and anticipation as they embarked on the journey that would ultimately lead to the liberation of their homeland. As they approached the outskirts of Mecca, Muhammad received word that the Quraysh had violated the terms of the treaty and mobilized their forces to confront the Muslims.

Undeterred by the Quraysh's betrayal, Muhammad remained resolute in his determination to reclaim Mecca for Islam. With a force of approximately 10,000 men, Muhammad and his companions entered Mecca under the cover of darkness, catching their adversaries by surprise and overwhelming them with their sheer numbers and determination.

The conquest of Mecca was not marked by bloodshed or violence, but rather by a spirit of forgiveness, reconciliation, and mercy. Despite years of persecution and hostility, Muhammad chose to extend clemency to his former adversaries, offering them amnesty and inviting them to embrace Islam. This act of magnanimity and forgiveness laid the foundation for the peaceful integration of Mecca into the burgeoning Muslim community and paved the way for the eventual spread of Islam throughout the Arabian Peninsula.

The conquest of Mecca was a watershed moment in the history of Islam—a triumph of faith, perseverance, and divine guidance that affirmed Muhammad's status as the chosen messenger of God and solidified the position of Islam as a dominant force in Arabia. Through his leadership and strategic acumen, Muhammad transformed a once-persecuted and marginalized community into a thriving and influential civilization that would shape the course of history for centuries to come.

The conquest of Mecca serves as a timeless reminder of the transformative power of faith, forgiveness, and reconciliation in the face of adversity. It stands as a testament to the enduring legacy of Prophet Muhammad and his companions, whose unwavering commitment to their cause and steadfast adherence to the principles of justice and compassion laid the foundation for a global faith community that continues to inspire millions around the world today.

8.5 Battle of Hunayn

In the tumultuous tapestry of early Islamic history, the Battle of Hunayn occupies a significant chapter—a momentous clash that tested the resolve, faith, and military prowess of Prophet Muhammad and his companions. Born out of the aftermath of the conquest of Mecca and the shifting alliances of the Arabian tribes, the Battle of Hunayn would come to symbolize the challenges and triumphs of the Muslim community as they sought to establish Islam as a dominant force in the Arabian Peninsula.

The Battle of Hunayn was sparked by the resistance of the Hawazin tribe, who, along with their allies from the Thaqif tribe, sought to challenge the burgeoning power of the Muslim community in the aftermath of the conquest of Mecca. Faced with the threat of a formidable coalition of tribes determined to thwart their advance, Muhammad and his companions mobilized their forces and set out to confront their adversaries on the battlefield.

The Muslim army, bolstered by their recent victory in Mecca and their unwavering faith in their cause, marched confidently towards Hunayn—a valley located northeast of Mecca—where the Hawazin and Thaqif forces had gathered in preparation for battle. Yet, despite their numerical superiority and superior weaponry, the Muslims found themselves facing a formidable adversary, as the Hawazin and Thaqif tribes launched a fierce assault against them.

In the initial stages of the battle, the Muslim forces were caught off guard by the ferocity of the enemy's attack, and a temporary rout ensued as panic and confusion gripped their ranks. Yet, in the midst of the chaos and turmoil, Muhammad remained steadfast in his resolve, rallying his companions and urging them to stand firm in the face of adversity.

With his leadership and guidance, the Muslim forces regrouped and launched a counterattack against their adversaries, turning the tide of battle in their favor. Through their unity, determination, and unwavering faith in God, the Muslims emerged victorious, routing the Hawazin and Thaqif forces and securing a decisive triumph that reaffirmed their status as the dominant power in the Arabian Peninsula.

The Battle of Hunayn was not merely a military victory; it was a testament to the resilience, faith, and unwavering commitment of the early Muslim community to their cause. For the Muslims, it served as a powerful reminder of the importance of steadfastness and perseverance in the face of adversity, and a reaffirmation of their faith in the guidance and leadership of Prophet Muhammad.

The aftermath of the Battle of Hunayn saw the consolidation of Muslim power in the Arabian Peninsula, as the defeated tribes submitted to the authority of Muhammad and embraced Islam. The spoils of war from the battle—including vast quantities of booty and prisoners of war—were distributed among the Muslim community, further strengthening their cohesion and unity.

Ultimately, the Battle of Hunayn stands as a timeless testament to the enduring legacy of courage, faith, and perseverance that defines the early Muslim community. It serves as a reminder of the transformative power of faith and unity in the face of adversity, and a powerful testament to the leadership and guidance of Prophet Muhammad in guiding his companions through the trials and tribulations of their journey.

Chapter 9: The Legacy

Prophet Muhammad, the founder of Islam, stands as one of the most influential figures in human history. His legacy and impact reverberate through the centuries, shaping the course of civilizations, inspiring countless millions, and leaving an indelible mark on the world as we know it. From his teachings of compassion and justice to his unwavering commitment to spreading the message of Islam, Muhammad's life and actions continue to resonate with people of all backgrounds and beliefs, transcending time and space to touch the hearts and minds of humanity.

Born in the city of Mecca in the year 570 CE, Muhammad grew up in a society plagued by ignorance, idolatry, and injustice. Yet, even in the midst of such darkness, he was known for his honesty, integrity, and compassion—a shining beacon of light amidst the shadows of ignorance and oppression.

In the Cave of Hira, Muhammad received his first revelation from God through the Angel Gabriel—a momentous event that would change the course of history forever. Over the next 23 years, Muhammad continued to receive divine revelations, which were compiled into the holy book of Islam, the Quran. Through his teachings, Muhammad sought to guide humanity towards the path of righteousness and submission to the will of God, calling upon people to worship one God and to live lives of compassion, justice, and mercy.

One of the key aspects of Muhammad's legacy is his role as a social reformer and champion of human rights. In a society rife with inequality, oppression, and exploitation, Muhammad sought to uplift the downtrodden and marginalized members of society, including orphans, widows, slaves, and the poor. He abolished the practice of infanticide, which was common in pre-Islamic Arabia, and established principles of social justice and equality that laid the foundation for a more just and compassionate society.

Muhammad's teachings also had a profound impact on the status of women in society. In a patriarchal society where women were often treated as property and denied basic rights and freedoms, Muhammad elevated the status of women and emphasized their inherent dignity and worth. He granted women the right to inherit property, enter into contracts, and seek divorce, and he encouraged their participation in public life and education. Through his teachings and example, Muhammad challenged the entrenched misogyny of his time and laid the groundwork for greater gender equality and empowerment.

Another aspect of Muhammad's legacy is his role as a peacemaker and diplomat. Despite facing relentless persecution and hostility from his adversaries, Muhammad consistently sought to resolve conflicts through peaceful means whenever possible. He negotiated treaties and alliances with neighboring tribes, mediated disputes among his followers, and demonstrated a willingness to forgive and reconcile with his enemies. The Treaty of Hudaybiyyah, in which Muhammad negotiated a truce with the Quraysh tribe of Mecca, is a prime example of his commitment to peace and diplomacy.

Perhaps the most enduring aspect of Muhammad's legacy is the global impact of Islam, the religion he founded. From its humble beginnings in the Arabian Peninsula, Islam spread rapidly across the world, encompassing diverse cultures, languages, and civilizations. Muhammad's message of monotheism, social justice, and moral integrity resonated with people from all walks of life, inspiring them to embrace Islam and adopt its teachings as a guiding light in their lives.

Today, Islam is the second-largest religion in the world, with over a billion followers spanning every corner of the globe. The principles of Islam, as articulated by Muhammad, continue to shape the lives and societies of millions of people, providing them with a framework for ethical living, spiritual fulfillment, and social justice. From the architecture of mosques to the rhythms of daily prayer, from the poetry of Rumi to the philosophy of Ibn Rushd, the influence of Muhammad and his teachings can be felt in every aspect of Islamic civilization.

In conclusion, Prophet Muhammad's legacy and impact on history are truly monumental. From his teachings of compassion and justice to his role as a social reformer and peacemaker, Muhammad's life and actions continue to inspire and uplift humanity to this day. Through his example of humility, kindness, and devotion to God, Muhammad exemplified the highest ideals of human excellence, leaving behind a legacy that will endure for eternity.

Chapter 10 : Why Muhammad was Chosen?

The question of why Muhammad was chosen by God as a messenger is a profound one, steeped in theological significance and divine mystery. Islamic tradition teaches that God's choice of Muhammad as His final messenger was part of His divine plan for humanity—a plan that unfolded over the course of history to guide and enlighten humanity.

There are several key reasons why Muhammad is believed to have been chosen as the messenger of God:

1. Exemplary Character: Muhammad was known for his impeccable character, honesty, integrity, and compassion. He was renowned for his trustworthiness and fairness, earning him the title of "Al-Amin" (the trustworthy) among his peers. His exemplary conduct and moral integrity made him a fitting vessel for delivering God's message to humanity.

There is one best example of his fairness (Al Amin), Even before Muhammad received his prophetic mission, he was known as "Al-Amin" (the trustworthy) among the people of Mecca. One notable incident that showcased his integrity occurred when the tribes of Mecca were rebuilding the Kaaba. They disagreed on who should have the honor of placing the Black Stone in its designated spot. To resolve the dispute, they agreed to let the first person to enter the Kaaba decide. When Muhammad entered, he proposed a solution that satisfied everyone: he placed the Black Stone on a cloak and asked each tribe to lift a corner of the cloak together, allowing them all to participate in the placement. This act demonstrated Muhammad's wisdom, diplomacy, and commitment to fairness.

2. Spiritual Preparedness: Before receiving the first revelation from God, Muhammad spent years in deep spiritual contemplation and reflection. He frequently retreated to the Cave of Hira, seeking solitude and divine guidance. His spiritual preparedness and receptivity made him uniquely attuned to receiving God's message and carrying out His divine will.

3. Mercy to Mankind: Muhammad's mission as a messenger of God was characterized by mercy and compassion towards all of humanity. He was sent as a "mercy to the worlds" (Quran 21:107), tasked with delivering a message of peace, justice, and guidance to people of all backgrounds and beliefs. His message emphasized the importance of compassion, forgiveness, and empathy towards others.

4. Seal of the Prophets: In Islamic belief, Muhammad is considered the Seal of the Prophets, meaning that he is the final prophet sent by God to convey His message to humanity. His prophethood completes and perfects the line of prophets that came before him, culminating in a comprehensive and final guidance for all of humanity until the end of time.

Ultimately, the reasons for Muhammad's selection as a messenger of God are known only to God Himself. From an Islamic perspective, Muhammad's prophethood is a manifestation of God's wisdom, mercy, and divine will, serving as a beacon of guidance and enlightenment for all of humanity. His life and teachings continue to inspire millions of people around the world, underscoring the timeless relevance and universal appeal of his message of faith, compassion, and devotion to God.

"With all these qualities, he became the final messenger of God on Earth, as per Islamic belief. Hence, he is now referred to as Prophet Muhammad, peace be upon him."

Thus concludes the tale of "Why He Was Chosen"—a story of faith, courage, and the enduring power of love.

Hope you had a great time reading this book...

Why was He Chosen?

(A Life of Prophet Muhammad)

Sadhu Prasad

Publisher
Fantabulous Publishers India
www.fantabulous.co.in[1]

Edition: 2024

---

1. http://www.fantabulous.co.in

Why was He Chosen?
Penned by Sadhu Prasad
Published by Fantabulous Publishers India

Popular Story and Activity Books for Children

Fanta-Award Recipients

(All Books available on Amazon-Worldwide and in Google as eBook)